moments of meditation

friends are a blessing

Emilie Barnes & Donna Otto

with **Anne Christian Buchanan**

Harvest House Publishers
Eugene, Oregon

Friends Are a Blessing
Copyright © 2000 by Harvest House Publishers
Eugene, Oregon 97402

ISBN 0-7369-0192-2

Text is adapted from *Friends of the Heart* by Emilie Barnes
and Donna Otto (Harvest House Publishers, 1999).

Design and production by
Left Coast Design, Portland, Oregon
Artwork by Gwendolyn Babbitt

Printed in China.

00 01 02 03 04 05 06 07 08 09 / PP / 10 9 8 7 6 5 4 3 2 1

Among all the relationships that define our lives, there is something special about friendship. Our friendships reveal who we are, even as they shape the people we will be. So cherish your friends. Hold them close. Seek them out, enjoy their company, and honor them with your care, your energy, and your appreciation. And as you treasure them, your life will be showered with blessings.

What is there about a good friend that makes her so special? Sometimes the simplest answer is the most profound: You like her. You feel better when she's around. Her presence refreshes you.

Thank you for giving me something no one else could—yourself.

HEATHER LYNCH

Let me benefit from you in the Lord; refresh my heart in Christ.

PHILEMON 20

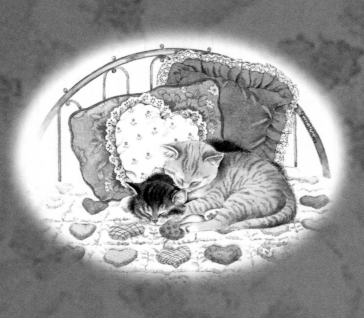

*R*ituals and traditions are part of any long-term relationship. A shared history is built in part on a foundation of "we always do this" together. Whatever you do, the real joy, of course, is having evergreen friends to always do it with.

You have always been with me,
and all that is mine is yours.

LUKE 15:31

A mature, life-long friendship is one of life's supreme accomplishments, as well as one of life's most astonishing gifts. As your friendships grow, you get better at being a friend.

*It is easy to say how we love new friends,
and what we think of them, but words can never
trace out all the fibers that knit us to the old.*

GEORGE ELIOT

There is a friend who sticks closer than a brother.

PROVERBS 18:24

Gwendolyn
Babbitt ©

What kind of lessons can friends teach us? Lessons in patience, lessons in assertiveness, lessons in generosity, how-to lessons for work and home. How to enjoy each other. How to care for one another. How to learn together and keep on learning.

Let us consider how to stimulate
one another to love and good deeds.

HEBREWS 10:24

Anyone you meet can help you grow. But we tend to learn the most from the people we trust the most. And that's why we can learn so much from our friends. We teach each other as we grow together.

Therefore encourage one another, and build up one another, just as you also are doing.

1 THESSALONIANS 5:11

Gwendolyn Babbitt

And he will be like a tree planted by streams
of water, which yields its fruit in its season,
and its leaf does not wither; and in
whatever he does, he prospers.

PSALM 1:3

*I*f friendships are gardens, then some friendships are annuals. They bloom for only a season, bringing joy, coloring our lives. Other friendships are perennials, the faithful, dependable blooms that return to our lives again and again. And then there are evergreens, persistently fresh, ever fragrant.

You are as welcome as flowers in May.

CHARLES MACKLIN

Fervently love one another from the heart.

1 PETER 1:22

*I*t's the little, thoughtful touches that keep your garden growing. It's the big, extravagant over-the-top gestures that twine your hearts together forever. Think: a daisy a day…and sometimes a roomful of roses.

❧

I am glad that in the springtime of life there were those who planted flowers of love in my heart.

ROBERT LOUIS STEVENSON

Kept promises fertilize our friend-ships. It is faithfulness in the little things. You are caring for your friendship when you show up for your coffee date, when you think twice about canceling your walk together, when you make a note to pray for your friend.

He who is faithful in a very little thing is faithful also in much.

LUKE 16:10

Encourage one another day after day.

HEBREWS 3:13

Most of the time, a little everyday maintenance is all you need to keep a friendship growing. A phone call. An e-mail. A quick visit and a chat and a promise to get together again soon. A thoughtful gift. A silly surprise.

A friendship can weather most things and thrive in thin soil—but it needs a little mulch of letters and phone calls and small silly presents every so often— just to save it from drying out completely.

PAM BROWN

How do you take care of a friendship? A lot of it comes naturally. As you spend time together and enjoy each other and help one another, chances are you are also taking care of each other and nurturing your friendship.

What brings joy to the heart is not so much the friend's gift as the friend's love.

ALFRED OF RIEVAULX

Be devoted to one another in brotherly love.

ROMANS 12:10

In a sense, it is the very act of caring for our friendships that make them so precious to us. We tend to love those things in which we have invested our time, our energies, our money, and our efforts.

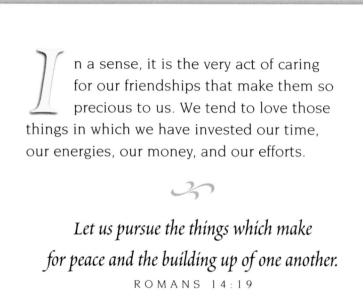

Let us pursue the things which make for peace and the building up of one another.

ROMANS 14:19

A friend loves at all times.

PROVERBS 17:17

aring for each other is one of the basic purposes of friendship. We all need the encouragement, the understanding, the advocacy that a friendship brings us. We all need the assurance that we are worth some trouble.

There is nothing better than the encouragement of a good friend.

KATHARINE BUTLER HATHAWAY

Comparing friendship to a garden is a wonderful way to envision such a close relationship. We plant seeds and weed. We water and fertilize. We work carefully to make our relationships lovely, leafy, living, and life-giving.

꙳

To each one of us friendship has a different meaning.
For all of us it is a gift. Friendship needs to be cherished
and nurtured. It needs to be cultivated on a daily basis.
Then shall it germinate and yield its fruit.

SOURCE UNKNOWN

You will be like a watered garden, and like a
spring of water whose waters do not fail.

ISAIAH 58:11

Gwendolyn Babbitt ©

T here's something about working side by side that builds friendship like nothing else can. It builds shared history. In fact, there is no better way to learn a person's true character than to see her on the job.

But the priests were too few...

therefore their brothers the Levites helped

them until the work was completed.

2 CHRONICLES 29:34

Two are better than one because they have a good return for their labor. For if either of them falls, the one will lift up [her] companion.

ECCLESIASTES 4:9,10

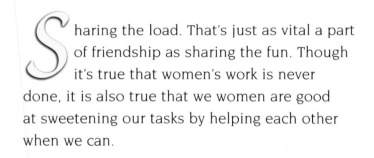

*S*haring the load. That's just as vital a part of friendship as sharing the fun. Though it's true that women's work is never done, it is also true that we women are good at sweetening our tasks by helping each other when we can.

Friendship is warmth in cold, firm ground in a bog.

MILES FRANKLIN

*S*illiness adds a special quality to the fun in friendship. It takes a lot of trust to let down your guard and be truly silly, even with someone you love. When you feel free to act absolutely silly with a friend, you understand the freedom friendship can grant.

*And you shall know
the truth, and the truth
shall make you free.*

JOHN 8:32

Celebration is part of friendship. Celebrate milestones. Celebrate accomplishments. Celebrate enthusiastically and extravagantly. Celebrate the fact that it is a beautiful day and you are friends.

This is the day which the Lord has made; let us rejoice and be glad in it.

PSALM 118:24

Gwendolyn Babbitt ©

*L*aughter is a healing, restorative part of the fun that comes with friendship. Our best friends, we find, are the ones we can laugh with. Laughter helps keep things warm and joyful, even in the midst of pain.

Then our mouth was filled with laughter,

and our tongue with joyful shouting.

PSALM 126:2

All friendship
is a joint creation
—a beautiful thing
created over time, together. Friendship
is crafted from the simplest materials: our
words and our silences and our silliness and
our sacrifice and our gifts and our gestures.
You give. I take. Then we switch places.

Greater love has no one than this,
that one lay down his life for his friends.

JOHN 15:13

Friendship is the pleasing
game of interchanging praise.

OLIVER WENDELL HOLMES

But I have called you friends...

JOHN 15:15

*O*ne of the most beautiful things about friendship is that it transcends categories and roles. You never know when a mother, sister, pastor's wife, or coworker will step over the line of labels and sign up as a treasured friend of the heart.

*She who finds a faithful
friend, finds a treasure.*

JEWISH PROVERB

"F riends of the heart" are unforgettable people who, for whatever reason, stake a permanent claim there. These are our chosen sisters—the ones who leave us pondering what we did to deserve them. Best of all, they feel the same way about us.

The love of each one of you toward one another grows ever greater.

2 THESSALONIANS 1:3

A friend is one of
those people who
walk into our lives
and find a home
in our hearts.

AUTHOR UNKNOWN

There's something exhilarating about that feeling of "You're just like me!" It's a feeling of being understood, of being validated, of sharing something special. And it's a basic part of how we choose our friends.

Be of the same mind toward one another.

ROMANS 12:16

Gwendolyn Babbitt ©

*F*riendship isn't like caviar and chocolate—delicious, but optional. It's more like juicy, delicious fruit—flavorful, nutritious, and absolutely necessary to happy, healthy living.

Dear friend, I am praying that all is well with you and that your body is as healthy as I know your soul is.

3 JOHN 2 TLB

Friends help us remember who we are and what we are about in life. They bring us insight and identity. They tell us the truth and challenge us to reach beyond ourselves. They believe in us.

Blessed is the influence of one true, loving soul on another.

GEORGE ELIOT

Therefore. . .speak truth, each one of you, with his neighbor, for we are members of one another.

EPHESIANS 4:25

Gwendolen
Babbitt ©

*O*ur friends are our lifelines, our sanity-savers, our reminders of who we are beyond the roles we play. We need them to grow, to be whole, to lead fruitful and productive and satisfying lives.

As each one has received a special gift, employ it in serving one another, as good stewards of the manifold grace of God.

1 PETER 4:10

The hallmark of true friendship is this: Whatever it is your friend gives to you, you want to give it back to her. The kind of friend she is to you, you want to be for her: loving, giving, trusting, laughing, and crying.

Then Jonathan made a covenant with David because he loved him as himself.

1 SAMUEL 18:3

Oil and perfume make the heart glad, so a man's counsel is sweet to his friend.

PROVERBS 27:9

Day and night, a friend is there for you if you need her. She is willing to give you her time, her energy, her insights, her possessions. She shares words and silences. She cries for you and shouts hurrah for you. She is free with her love and sympathy.

The best relationships…are built up like a fine lacquer finish, with accumulated layers made of many little acts of love.

GILBERT AND BRADSHAW

Some friendships are as comforting and comfortable as a well-worn pair of shoes. Others are full of excitement and adventure. The best ones are laced with laughter and softened with tears and strengthened with a spiritual bond.

For I have come to have much joy and comfort in your love.

PHILEMON 7

Great is my confidence in you, great is my
boasting on your behalf; I am filled with comfort.

2 CORINTHIANS 7:4

*T*rust is the sweet, solid foundation in your relationship with a friend. You trust her to hold close the private things you reveal to her. Your bedrock confidence is that she truly wants the best for you, whatever that best may be.

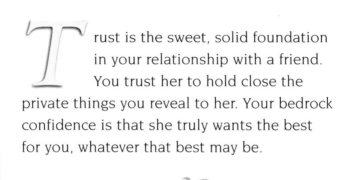

Few delights can equal the mere presence of one whom we utterly trust.

GEORGE MACDONALD

friend is sensitive to the person you are. She listens both to the words you say and to the ones you don't say. She sees you, and she loves what she sees, and somehow you like yourself better when you're together.

~

Thy care has preserved my spirit.

JOB 10:12